COUNTRY MUSIC

"Any book without a mistake in it has
had too much money spent on it"
Sir William Collins, publisher

COUNTRY MUSIC

MIKE EVANS

ff&f

Country Music
Facts, Figures & Fun

Published by
Facts, Figures & Fun, an imprint of
AAPPL Artists' and Photographers' Press Ltd.
Church Farm House, Wisley, Surrey GU23 6QL
info@ffnf.co.uk www.ffnf.co.uk
info@aappl.com www.aappl.com

Sales and Distribution
UK and export: Turnaround Publisher Services Ltd.
orders@turnaround-uk.com
USA and Canada: Sterling Publishing Inc.
sales@sterlingpub.com
Australia & New Zealand: Peribo Pty.
peribomec@bigpond.com
South Africa: Trinity Books. trinity@iafrica.com

A catalogue record for this book is available from the
British Library.

ISBN 13: 9781904332534
ISBN 10: 1904332536

Design (contents and cover): Malcolm Couch
mal.couch@blueyonder.co.uk

Printed in China by Imago Publishing
info@imago.co.uk

CONTENTS

THE ROOTS OF COUNTRY MUSIC

The term country music refers to a variety of styles, originally popular among working class white Americans in the rural areas of the South and West.

Originally known by the derogatory label "hillbilly music", the term was replaced by country and western music in 1949 and eventually shortened to country music.

FROM THE OLD COUNTRY

But the origins of country music go way back a century before, to the waves of immigrants from the "Old Countries" of the British Isles, and what was later Eire. Their songs and dances, nursery rhymes and ballads, jigs and reels, would form the backbone of the folk musical tradition of rural America, and the basis for what became known as "old time" country music.

These roots of country music lie largely in the folk songs and instrumental music of the English, Irish, and Scots who settled in the Appalachian regions of the Mid-South during the eighteenth and nineteenth centuries. Many of these mountainous areas – stretching down through the Virginias, Kentucky, North Carolina and Tennessee – were not settled until the 1830s, and then by very poor immigrants. There subsequently evolved seemingly "backward" communities, cut off from the rest of America, still attached to their traditions but also preoccupied with the daily struggle for survival.

SONGS THAT CROSSED THE ATLANTIC

Some of the most famous and enduring folk songs of America had their orgins in Britain and Ireland.

Song	Area of Origin	Dating from
Froggie Went A-Courtin'	Scotland	16th century
Lord Randall	Scotland	16th century
The Foggy, Foggy Dew	Suffolk and West Country	16th century
Brennan On The Moor	Ireland	17th century
Barbara Allen	England, Scotland, Ireland	17th century
Lord Thomas And Fair Elinore	Scotland	18th century
Pretty Polly	England	18th century
Heart Of Oak	England	18th century

Other origins of country music can be traced back to the flamenco and habañera music of Spain, the polka and other dances of Eastern Europe and – as with virtually all the popular music of the United States – the influence of the slave populations shipped from the African continent. In fact one of the major instruments in Appalachian and early country music, the banjo, has its origins in Afro-American history.

BACKGROUND OF THE BANJO

Originally from Arabia, and brought to western Africa by the spread of Islam, the banjo then ended up in America. Its name is commonly thought to be derived from *mbanza,* a term in the Kimbundu pre-colonial language spoken by many of the peoples of central and west Africa. The banjo was largely denigrated as a "slave instrument" until it became popular via the Minstrel Shows, starting in the 1840s, a process hastened by its introduction to the Southern Mountains after the Civil War in the late 1860s.

TRADITIONAL INSTRUMENTS

The banjo was just one of the traditional instruments that were imported to the New World via various waves of immigrants.

Instrument	Area of Origin	Dating from
Dulcimer	Germany / Holland / Sweden / Spain	12th century
Banjo	Arabia / West Africa	15th century

Fiddle	Italy	16th century
Mandolin	Italy / Spain	16th century
Jew's Harp	England / Russia / Italy / Norway	16th century
Accordion	Germany / Austria	19th century
Concertina	England	19th century
Harmonica	Germany	19th century
Autoharp	Germany	19th century

The other crucial element in "old time" music was the gospel song. Again, handed down in the main by settlers from the British Isles, 19th century hymns provided the core of the tradition, as they also did for Black American gospel music. Indeed, the latter has much in common with its white conterpart in the structure of the songs, harmony singing and sheer exhuberance of delivery.

Two publishing events in the early part of the 20th century sparked a widespread interest in America's white musical heritage and "old time" music. First, in 1910, the musicologist John Lomax published *Cowboy Songs and Other Frontier Ballads*. Then in 1916 the English song collector Cecil Sharp put together a collection of folk music from the Appalachian mountains – or, to be more accurate, the Cumberland Mountains at the border between Kentucky and Tennessee.

But it wasn't until 1922, when Texas fiddler Eck Robertson cut the first record of "old-time" (or "old timey") music, that the popularity of what also became known as "hillbilly" really began to take off, via pioneering artists, record labels and radio stations.

HOLLYWOOD COUNTRY

Country music has provided the theme to a number of big-screen movies by distinguished directors, the latest at the time of writing being the Johnny Cash biopic *Walk The Line* starring Joaquin Phoenix as Cash, Reese Witherspoon as his wife June Carter Cash and country singer Shelby Lynne in an outstanding performance as Cash's mother Carrie.

Title / Director / Subject

Nashville [1975] Robert Altman

Music City-based melodrama

Coal Miner's Daughter [1980] Michael Apted

Loretta Lynn biopic

Rhinestone [1984] Bob Clark

Dolly Parton as a country star who turns a New York cab driver into a singer to win a bet

Sweet Dreams [1985] Karel Reisz

Patsy Cline biopic

Pure Country [1992] Christopher Cain

Country star George Strait plays a singer who goes back to his roots

Walk The Line [2005] James Mangold

Johnny Cash biopic

OLD TIMEY MUSIC & BLUEGRASS

··············· THE RADIO REVOLUTION ···············

Even before the first hillbilly songs were released on record, it was the phenomenal spread of radio in the early Twenties that gave country music its earliest popular outlet.

In 1922, two years after the debut of commercial radio in America, a station based in Georgia (WSB) became the first to broadcast old-time songs to its audience. It was followed in 1923 by WBAP in Forth Worth, Texas, which launched the first-ever "barn dance" show, and in 1924, the Chicago radio station WLS began broadcasting a similar programme – *National Barn Dance* – that could be heard throughout the Midwest. Then in 1925 Nashville's first radio station (WSM) began broadcasting a barn dance that would eventually change its name to the *Grand Ole Opry* and become the most famous and longest-running country music broadcast of all time.

GRAND OLE OPRY TIMELINE

Celebrating its 80th anniversary in 2005, Nashville's *Grand Old Opry* has been at the forefront of promoting country music's greatest talents throughout the music's history

1925: The National Life and Accident Insurance Company open a radio station in Nashville with the call-sign WSM based on the company motto "We Shield Millions"

1925: WSM launches *WSM Barn Dance*

1927: The hugely popular *Barn Dance* renamed the *Grand Ole Opry*

1932: The station increases its output to 50,000 watts, enabling most of the United States and parts of Canada to tune into the *Opry* every Saturday night

1939: Its popularity is boosted again when the coast-to-coast NBC Radio Network begins carrying the show

1943: The Opry relocates to a former Nashville religious meeting house built in 1892, the Ryman Auditorium, to accomodate the huge demand for "live audience" tickets

1947: Ernest Tubb takes a group of Opry stars to New York's Carnegie Hall

1949: The Opry's first European tour, with Red Foley, Roy Acuff, Minnie Pearl, Hank Williams and others visiting U.S. military bases in England, Germany, and the Azores

1955: Ralston Purina begins sponsoring an hour-long regional-network TV show from the Ryman stage featuring Opry stars

1974: The Opry moves from the Ryman to be the heart of a multi-million-dollar entertainment complex nine miles from downtown Nashville

1978: The national PBS Television Network broadcasts the show on March 4, and annually through to 1981

1985: A half-hour TV segment of the Opry begins airing each Saturday night on TNN as *Grand Ole Opry Live*

2006: Radio is still important, as the two-hour show *America's Grand Ole Opry Weekend* is syndicated in some 200 markets via the Internet, satellite radio and terrestrial networks

RECORD PIONEERS

The very first commercial recordings of country music were made on June 30, 1922, at the studios of the Victor Talking Machine Company in New York City. They were a pair of fiddle duets by the Texan fiddler **Alexander "Eck" Robertson** and Henry C. Gilliand, 'Arkansas Traveler' and 'Turkey in the Straw'. The following day, Robertson cut six additional solo tracks, including the popular 'Sallie Gooden', plus two songs that were never released. Victor initially released 'Arkansas Traveler', backed with 'Sallie Gooden', on a limited basis in September 1922, putting the disc into general circulation in April 1923.

The record that more generally gets cited as the first country release, 'The Little Old Log Cabin In The Lane' b/w 'The Old Hen Cackled And The Rooster's Going to Crow', was made in June 1923 by Fiddlin' John Carson in Atlanta, Georgia, for the OKeh label. It came about almost by accident, when company executive **Ralph Peer** described Carson as 'terrible' and 'pluperfect awful', but it was released anyway and became an unexpected hit.

Peer was quick to capitalize on Carson's success and recorded a flood of music by the Hill Billies, the Stoneman Family, Vernon Dalhart, and other first-generation hillbilly names. He went on to discover country's first real stars – in fact two of the most important country acts of all time – Jimmie Rodgers and the Carter Family.

Profile: The Carter Family
A.P. Carter (vocals, fiddle)
Born: Alvin Pleasant Carter, 15 December 1891, Mace Springs, Virginia
Died: 7 November 1960, Mace Springs, Virginia
Sara Carter (vocals, guitar, autoharp)
Born: Sara Dougherty, 21 July 1899, Wise County, Virginia
Died: 8 January 1979, Lodi, California
Maybelle Carter (vocals, guitar, autoharp)
Born: Maybelle Addington, 10 May 1909, Copper Creek, Virginia
Died: 23 October 1978, Nashville, Tennessee

Recording Debut: August 1927, Bristol, Tennessee

Classic Records: Worried Man Blues; Wabash Cannonball; Will The Circle Be Unbroken; Wildwood Flower; I'm Thinking Tonight Of My Blue Eyes; Jimmy Brown The Newsboy; Keep On The Sunny Side; My Clinch Mountain Home; Foggy Mountain Top; Diamonds In The Rough; Lonesome Valley

Facts'n'Figures: Sara Dougherty married A.P. Carter in June 1915, and Maybelle Addington was her cousin, who married A.P's brother Ezra. Their biggest record, 'Wildwood Flower' [1928], sold around a million copies; they had learned the song orally in Virginia, (although it had been published back in 1860), and were paid just $75 dollars to record it. Altogether they wrote over 300 songs, and had recorded over 250 sides by the early Forties.

Although used as a derogatory description of mountain folk since the earliest years of the 20th century, the term "hillbilly" was first used in a musical context on 'Hill Billie Blues' by "Uncle" Dave Macon in 1924. Then in January 1925, when Ralph Peer was recording a new band, he asked what he should call the group. "We're nothing but a bunch of hillbillies from North Carolina and Virginia. Call us anything", came the reply, so Peer called them The Hill Billies.

TEN EARLY HILLBILLY HOTSHOTS
TITLE / ARTIST / YEAR

Arkansas Traveler
"Eck" Robertson / Henry C. Gilliand 1922
The Little Old Log Cabin In The Lane
Fiddlin' John Carson 1923
Hill Billie Blues
"Uncle" Dave Macon 1924
Wreck Of The Old 97
Vernon Dalhart 1924
When The Work's All Done This Fall
Carl Sprague 1925
The Titanic
Ernest Stoneman 1925
Don't Let Your Deal Go Down
Charile Poole/North Carolina Ramblers 1925
Worried Blues
Frank Hutchison 1926
Nine Pound Hammer
The Hill Billies 1927
Red River Valley
The Skillet Lickers 1927

Ralph Peer moved from the OKeh label to Victor at the end of 1925, and in August 1927 presided over an historic session in Bristol, Tennesse, making the debut records of the **Carter Family** and **Jimmie Rodgers**. These would be the two most influential names in the early development of country music. The Carters represented the folk and gospel 'mountain music' tradition, while Rodgers established the blues and even vaudeville elements in country.

Profile: Jimmie Rodgers (vocals, guitar)
Born: James Charles Rodgers, 8 September 1897, Meridan, Mississippi
Died: 26 May 1933, New York City

Recording Debut: August 1927, Bristol, Tennessee

Classic Records: Blue Yodel; Brakeman's Blues; Yodelling Cowboy; My Old Pal; Waiting For A Train; Looking For A New Mama; Pistol Packin' Papa; Muleskinner Blues; Blue Yodel No 9

Facts'n'Figures: A former employee of the Mobile & Ohio Railroad, Rodgers was known as "The Singing Brakeman", and was credited with introducing yodelling to country music. His first big hit 'Blue Yodel' [1928] sold over half a million copies, and 'Blue Yodel No 9', recorded in Hollywood in 1930 – by which time he was country's first superstar – included Louis Armstrong on trumpet.

THE *O BROTHER WHERE ART THOU?* PHENOMENON

The 1998 film *O Brother Where Art Thou?*, directed by Joel and Ethan Coen, heralded a revival of interest in old timey and bluegrass music, with a soundtrack that featured vintage tracks alongside modern performances of old hillbilly material by contemporary artsists including Alison Krauss, Gillian Welch, Norman Blake, John Hartford and Emmylou Harris. The film includes no less than four versions of what can be considered the theme song of the movie, 'I Am A Man Of Constsant Sorrow', a traditional song which first appeared in printed form in 1913, and on record in 1928 by Emry Arthur on the Vocalion label.

O Brother Where Art Thou? **Soundtrack**
(vintage recordings dated)

Po Lazarus James Carter & the Prisoners [1959]
Big Rock Candy Mountain
Harry Kirby McClintock [1928]
You Are My Sunshine Norman Blake
Down To The River To Pray Alison Krauss
I Am A Man Of Constant Sorrow
The Soggy Bottom Boys
Hard Time Killing Floor Blues
Chris Thomas King
I Am A Man Of Constant Sorrow
Norman Blake
Keep On The Sunny Side The Whites
I'll Fly Away Gillian Welch and Alison Krauss
Didn't Leave Nobody But The Baby
Emmylou Harris, Alison Krauss and Gillian Welch
In The Highways
Sarah, Hannah and Leah Peasall

I Am Weary (Let Me Rest) The Cox Family
I Am A Man Of Constant Sorrow John Hartford
O Death Ralph Stanley
In The Jailhouse Now The Soggy Bottom Boys
I Am A Man of Constant Sorrow
The Soggy Bottom Boys
Indian War Whoop John Hartford
Lonesome Valley Fairfield Four
Angel Band The Stanley Brothers [1955]

So great was the impact of the music in the movie that a live tour was staged, labelled 'Down From The Mountain', featuring Emmylou Harris, Alison Krauss, Chris Thomas King, the Cox Family, Gillian Welch and others who had featured in the film.

THE SOUND OF BLUEGRASS

Closely identified with 'old timey' music, bluegrass could be said to represent hillbilly music coming of age, certainly on a commercial level. It shared with hillbilly its roots in Appalachian music, but with more evidence of the influence of jazz and blues. Like a lot of jazz, bluegrass features the instruments taking it in turn to play lead with the others backing, as opposed to the more ensemble appoach of old timey music.

Like hillbilly music, bluegrass features mostly acoustic stringed instruments including the fiddle, banjo, acoustic guitar, mandolin, and upright bass (which is occasionally substituted by an electric bass). A regular item in bluegrass line-ups is the resonator guitar, usually known by its brand name, the Dobro.

Vocally, bluegrass is distinguished by two, three or four part harmonies with an emphasis on the highest voice – what has been termed the "high lonesome sound."

Bluegrass developed in the Forties, and can be said to have started with the formation of **Bill Monroe**'s Bluegrass Boys (whence it derived its name) in 1939. Monroe's band of 1945-1948, which featured banjo player **Earl Scruggs** and guitarist **Lester Flatt**, has remained the classic template for bluegrass music to this day.

Profile: Bill Monroe (vocals, mandolin)
Born: William Smith Monroe, 13 September 1911, Rosine, Kentucky
Died: 9 September 1996, Springfield, Tennessee

Recording Debut: February 1936

Classic Records: Orange Blossom Special; Kentucky Waltz; Blue Moon of Kentucky; Footprints In The Snow; Molly And Tenbrooks; Alabama Waltz; Blue Grass Breakdown; Scotland; Mule Skinner Blues

Facts'n'Figures:
In 1970, Bill Monroe was elected to the Country Music Hall of Fame in Nashville. The following year the Nashville Songwriters Association elected him to their Hall of Fame, and in 1991 Bill was inducted into the International Bluegrass Music Hall of Honor. He was awarded the Lifetime Achievement Award by the National Association of Recording Arts and Sciences in 1993, and was presented with the National Medal of the Arts in 1995 by President Bill Clinton.

When they left Bill Monroe in 1948, Flatt and Scruggs became even bigger stars in their own right, fronting one of the most potent bluegrass outfits ever, the Foggy Mountain Boys. They attracted wordwide attention in 1967, when their 'Foggy Mountain Breakdown' was featured on the soundtrack of the movie *Bonnie and Clyde*.

Profile: Flatt and Scruggs
Lester Flatt (guitar, vocal)
Born: Lester Raymond Flatt, 28 June 1914, Overton County, Tennessee
Died: 11 May 1979, Nashville, Tennessee
Earl Scruggs (banjo, vocal)
Born: Earl Eugene Scruggs, 6 January 1924, Flint Hill, North Carolina

Recording Debut: Fall 1948, Knoxville, Tennessee

Classic Records: 'Tis Sweet To Be Remembered; Foggy Mountain Breakdown; Jimmy Brown The Newsboy; Cabin On The Hill; Ballad of Jed Clampett; Crying My Heart Out Over You; Pearl Pearl Pearl; You Are My Flower; Petticoat Junction; New York Town; Nashville Cats; California Uptight Band

Facts'n'Figures:
After being shunned by the *Grand Ole Opry* when they left Bill Monroe, in 1953 Flatt and Scruggs secured a morning show on WSM radio in Nashville, the same station that hosted the *Opry*, and in 1955 they were finally invited to join the *Opry* regulars "by popular demand". They also began a series of TV programmes in various Appalachian towns, and in 1957 their *Foggy*

Mountain Jamboree was the first bluegrass album devoted to a single band.

The other founding fathers of bluegrass in what is rightly regarded its "Golden Age" of the Fifties and Sixties included the **Stanley Brothers** (who broke through in 1948 with their band the Clinch Mountain Boys), Reno and Smiley, Jim & Jesse, the Blue Sky Boys and the Osbourne Brothers.

TEN BLUEGRASS BESTSELLERS

Bill Monroe	Blue Moon of Kentucky	1946
Blue Sky Boys	Kentucky	1947
Don Reno / Arthur Smith	Feuding Banjos	1955
Osbourne Brothers	Once More	1958
Jimmy Martin	Rock Hearts	1958
Stanley Brothers	How Far To Little Rock	1960
Flatt and Scruggs	Ballad of Jed Clampett	1962
Jim and Jesse	Diesel On My Trail	1967
Flatt and Scruggs	Foggy Mountain Breakdown	1967
Eric Weissberg / Steve Mandell	Dueling Banjos	1968

Bluegrass has never been far away from mainstream music. Sixties folk-rock outfit the Dillards took the bluegrass sound to a whole new young audience. And in the Nineties, Ricky Scaggs, who had started off as a bluegrass musician before crossing over to a more broad-based style in the Eighties, returned to bluegrass with his band Kentucky Thunder. At the same time world-famous country names including Patty Loveless and Dolly Parton returned to their "mountain roots" with influential bluegrass albums.

BLUEGRASS ON THE BIG SCREEN

1967 BONNIE AND CLYDE
(director Arthur Penn)
Music: Foggy Mountain Breakdown / Flatt and Scruggs

1972 DELIVERANCE
(director John Boorman)
Music: Dueling Banjos / Eric Weissberg and Steve Mandell

1976 HARLAN COUNTY, USA
(documentary, director Barbara Kopple)
Music: Merle Travis

2000 O BROTHER WHERE ART THOU?
(director Joel & Ethan Coen)
Music: Various including Alison Krauss, Emmylou Harris etc.

2003 COLD MOUNTAIN
(director Anthony Minghella)
Music: Alison Krauss, Cassie Franklin etc, five songs by Jack White

Much of the increased awareness of bluegrass world-wide has been helped by its inclusion in a number of Hollywood films over the years. After the huge success of *O Brother Where Art Thou?* the music enjoyed a genuine revival spearheaded by the likes of Alison Krauss and Union Station, Gillian Welch and Norman Blake. Also prominent though less high-profile are "progressive" (or "newgrass") outfits such as the Yonder Mountain String Band, and the virtuoso banjo player Béla Fleck with his band the Flecktones.

SIX OF THE BEST CONTEMPORARY BLUEGRASS ALBUMS

1996 Gary Brewer & The Kentucky Ramblers
Goin' Back to Kentucky

1999 Blue Highway
Blue Highway

2000 Rhonda Vincent
Back Home Again

2000 Nickel Creek
Nickel Creek

2001 Alison Krauss & Union Station
New Favorite

2005 Norman and Nancy Blake
Back Home In Sulphur Springs

Singing Cowboys & Western Swing

THE SINGING COWBOYS

Western music, or cowboy music as it more popularly became known, had similar roots to Appalachian mountain music, in the folk ballads from England, Scotland and Ireland. Developing with settlers in the American and Canadian West, it often celebrated the exploits of frontiersmen, and later folk heroes such as Jesse James and Billy the Kid.

In the South-West states of Texas, Arizona, New Mexico and southern California, Mexican music also exerted a considerable influence, with the waltz and later the tango frequently evident.

Although popular on the 19th century vaudeville stage, western songs were first "officially" recognized in 1910 when the folk song collector John Lomax published *Cowboy Songs and Other Frontier Ballads*. But it was in the Twenties, with the mass spread of radio, that the first "singing cowboys" began to make their mark, with performers such as Carl Sprague, Goebel Reeves and Otto Gray.

TRADITIONAL WESTERN BALLADS THAT MADE IT BIG

Get Along Little Doggies
Year first a hit record: 1937
Popularised by: Gene Autry
Also popular by: Roy Rogers & the Sons of the Pioneers

Home On The Range
Year first a hit record: 1933
Popularised by: Bing Crosby
Also popular by: Sons of the Pioneers

Red River Valley
Year first a hit record: 1931
Popularised by: Peterson's Hobo Orchestra
Also popular by: Rocky Mountaineers, Andrews Sisters, Bing Crosby, Sons of the Pioneers

Streets of Laredo [aka 'A Cowboy's Lament']
Year first a hit record: 1949
Popularised by: Dick Haymes
Also popular by: Johnny Cash, Marty Robbins

Cowgirls got a look-in too, the biggest star by far being Patsy Montana. With her backing band the Prairie Ramblers she made a string of records, the most famous being her 1935 hit 'I Want To Be A Cowboy's Sweetheart'.

The other big female act was the duo of sisters Millie

and Dolly Good known as the Girls Of The Golden
West. Via the radio show *National Barn Dance* (which
also included Patsy Montana and Gene Autry in its
roster of regulars) they enjoyed huge success with
such numbers as 'Ragtime Cowboy Joe', 'Lonesome
Cowgirl' and their signature 'Silvery Moon On The
Golden Gate'.

The Girls Of the Golden West claimed to be from
Texas, but in fact were farm girls from Illinois, working out of St Louis, Cincinnati and Chicago. And they
weren't the only outfit to embroider their "cowboy"
past; the Beverly Hill Billies were launched as a group
of "hick" singers apparently discovered in Beverly
Hills, but were actually put together by a local Los
Angeles radio station. When the TV show of the same
name was aired in the Sixties, the storyline (and title)
was so similar to the one concocted for the cowboy
band that ex-members of the latter sued the show's
producers.

SINGING COWBOYS
OF THE SILVER SCREEN

The big break-through for cowboy music came via
Hollywood with the advent of talking pictures.
Through the Thirties, Forties and Fifties a succession
of "singing cowboys" fronted hundreds of Western B-
movies.

The most famous of these was **Gene Autry**, closely
rivalled in the popularity stakes by **Roy Rogers**, while
other guitar-totin' gunslingers of the silver screen

included Ken Maynard, Tex Ritter, Rex Allen, and Monte Hale.

Gene Autry – who started broadcasting and making records as "Oklahoma's Yodellin' Cowboy" in the late Twenties – made his first film appearance in a Ken Maynard feature *In Old Santa Fe* in 1934 , and starred in his own fully-fledged musical Western in 1935's *Tumbling Tumbleweeds*. Usually with his horse Champion, he had starred in nearly a hundred feature films by the early Fifties. The movies, often with his sidekick from his radio shows Lester "Smiley" Burnette, promoted a string of hit records in the process.

Profile: Gene Autry (vocals, guitar)
Born: Orvon Autry, 29 September 1907, Tioga Springs, Texas
Died: 2 October 1998, Studio City, California

Recording Debut: 'My Dreaming Of You' / 'My Alabama Home', 1929

Classic Records: That Silver Haired Daddy Of Mine; Tumbling Tumbleweeds; Mexicali Rose; Back In The Saddle Again; South Of The Border; You Are My Sunshine; It Makes No Difference Now; Be Honest With Me; Tweedle-O-Twill; At Mail Call Today; Rudolph The Red-Nosed Reindeer

Facts'n'Figures: Autry made 635 recordings, including more than 300 songs written or co-written by him. His records sold more than 100 million copies and he has more than a dozen gold and platinum records, including the first record ever certified gold. 'That Silver Haired Daddy of Mine' [1931] eventually sold over five million copies, and Autry also had three other million-selling discs in 'Here Comes Santa Claus' [1947], 'Peter Cottontail' [1949], and the 9 million-seller 'Rudolph The Red Nosed Reindeer' in 1948, which was the second best-selling Christmas single of all time.

GENE AUTRY'S COWBOY CODE

Gene Autry kept to a stict personal moral code. He didn't drink, smoke, kiss his leading ladies, or shoot first in his movies. He even published a "Cowboy Code" for the guidance of his young fans.

1. The Cowboy must never shoot first, hit a smaller man, or take unfair advantage.
2. He must never go back on his word, or a trust confided in him.
3. He must always tell the truth.
4. He must be gentle with children, the elderly, and animals.
5. He must not advocate or possess racially or religiously intolerant ideas.
6. He must help people in distress.
7. He must be a good worker.
8. He must keep himself clean in thought, speech, action, and personal habits.
9. He must respect women, parents, and his nation's laws.
10. The Cowboy is a patriot.

Known as the "King of the Cowboys", Gene Autry's biggest rival on screen was Roy Rogers, although the latter never made as big an impact as Autry as far as music was concerned. He started out in the Twenties with groups that included the Rocky Mountaineers and the Hollywood Hillbillies, before forming what would be his most celebrated line-up, the Sons of the Pioneers.

Formed by Roy Rogers in 1933, the **Sons of the Pioneers** were hugely influential both with Rogers as front man (from 1933 to 1938) and after his departure. Their gentle close harmony became a hallmark of the "singing cowboy" style, and a string of hits included 'Tumbling Tumbleweeds' [1934], and 'Cool Water' in 1941, both written by member Bob Nolan, and 'Riders In The Sky' [1949].

Profile: Roy Rogers (vocals)
Born: Leonard Franklin Slye, 5 November 1911, Cincinnati, Ohio
Died: 6 July 1998, Apple Valley, California

Recording Debut: 'Way Out There', 1929

Classic Records: Hi-Yo Silver; Happy Trails To You; Think Of Me; Pecos Bill; Don't Fence Me In; Blue Shadows On The Trail; These Are The Good Old Days; Hoppy, Gene, And Me; A Four-Legged Friend; Ride, Concrete Cowboy, Ride

Facts'n'Figures: Roy Rogers starred in over 100 movies, and had his own TV show in the mid-Fifties. He recorded with RCA-Victor for many years, followed by Capitol, Word, 20th Century and MCA. In 1980 he and the Sons of the Pioneers teamed up once

COWBOY CROSS-OVERS

Ten "Western"-style songs that were huge hits in the mainstream market.

Cool Water
Composer: Bob Nolan
Versions included: Sons of the Pioneers [1941], Vaughan Monroe [1948], Frankie Laine [1955]

Deep In The Heart Of Texas
Composer: June Hershey / Don Swander
Versions included: Bing Crosby/ Woody Herman [1942]

Don't Fence Me In
Composer: Cole Porter
Versions included: Bing Crosby/ Andrews Sisters, Roy Rogers [both 1944]

High Noon (theme)
Composer: Ned Washington / Dimitri Tiomkin
Versions included: Tex Ritter, Frankie Laine [both 1952]

Home On The Range
Composer: trad arr. Ted Ezra
Versions included: Sons of the Pioneers, Bing Crosby [both 1933]

Mexacali Rose
Composer: Jack Teeney / Helen Stone
Versions included: Gene Autry [1936], Bing Crosby [1939], Slim Whitman [1961]

Mule Train
Composer: Johnny Lange / Hy Heath /
Fred Glickman
Versions included: Vaughan Monroe,
Tennessee Ernie Ford, Frankie Laine [all 1949]

Riders In The Sky
Composer: **Stan Jones**
Versions included: Vaughan Monroe [1949],
Ramrods [1961]

South Of The Border
Composer: Michael Carr / Jimmy Kennedy
Versions included: Gene Autry, Al Bowly [both
1939], Frank Sinatra [1953]

Yellow Rose Of Texas
Composer: Don George
Versions included: Mitch Miller [1955]

more for 'Ride, Concrete Cowboy, Ride' from the movie *Smokey and the Bandit II*. Inducted into the Country Music Hall of Fame in 1988, in 1991 he was back in the country charts with 'Hold On Partner', a duet with Clint Black from his *Tribute* album, in which the 80-year-old cowboy star duetted with current stars including Lorrie Morgan, Kathy Mattea, Ricky Van Shelton, Randy Travis, Restless Heart, and the Kentucky HeadHunters.

After he left the Sons of the Pioneers, Rogers' regular backing group were the Riders of the Purple Sage, after whom a country-rock band was named in the Seventies, the New Riders of the Purple Sage.

Along with his actress wife Dale Evans, who appeared in many of Rogers' films through the Forties and Fifties, the cowboy star's on-screen partners were his toothless sidekick George "Gabby" Hayes, and palamino horse Trigger. When Trigger died at the age of 33 in 1963, Roy had him stuffed and mounted outside his California home.

As well as actual "singing cowboys" like Autry and Rogers creating western hits via their movies, several best-sellers of the genre were notably used as theme songs for non-musical westerns. The most celebrated of these was the theme from the dramatic 1952 film *High Noon*, which **Tex Ritter** sang ("Do not forsake me, oh my darling...") on the soundtack. Although it was hit for Ritter, reaching Number 12 in *Billboard*, it became a chart-topper for Frankie Laine, and went on to win an Oscar for the best film song.

Other songs that were similarly promoted as movie themes included 'The Man From Laramie' sung by Al Martino [1955], the haunting 'Call Of The Faraway Hills' which accompanied the classic 1953 film *Shane*, the Oscar-winning 'Buttons and Bows' from the 1948 Bob Hope comedy *The Paleface* and even Marilyn Monroe singing the title song for 1954's *River Of No Return*.

HOW HAWAII GAVE COUNTRY MUSIC THE STEEL GUITAR

Popularised among hillbilly bands and western swing outfits during the Thirties, the pedal steel guitar had its roots in Hawaii. It was invented in Honolulu by Joseph Kekuku around 1885, and first became popular in the US when it was used as the incidental music to Richard Walton Tully's play *Bird of Paradise* in 1912. It got more exposure at the Hawaiian pavillion at the 'Panama Pacific Exhibition' in San Francisco in 1915, the same year that 'On The Beach At Waikiki', composed by Henry Kailimai and Sonny Cunha, started a nation-wide craze. All the major American record labels started having hits with Hawaiian music, including Sonny Cunha's 'Everybody Hula' [1916], Richard Whiting's 'Along the Way to Waikiki' [1917], and Walter Blaufuss' 'My Isle of Golden Dreams' in 1919. The craze subsided in the Twenties, but as it did, the sound of the steel guitar began to appear on cowboy records towards the end of the decade. Through the Thirties and Forties it became an established trademark of country music instrumentation.

WESTERN SWING

BIG BAND JAZZ GOES WEST

Emanating from Texas and Oklahoma during the big band era from the mid-Thirties to early Fifties, Western Swing was a form of country as hot dance music played in the context of a large swing-style band. "Country" instruments like steel guitars and fiddles were augmented by jazz-oriented saxophones and brass line-ups, playing arrangements injected with a strong blues feel and plenty of improvised solos all round.

The most popular and influential Western Swing outfit was fiddler Bob Wills and his Texas Playboys, while other big names included Milton Brown and his Musical Brownies, Spade Cooley, and Cliff Bruner's Texas Wanderers.

The first Bob Wills line-up was a quartet called the Wills Fiddle Band. Their first break came with a regular radio program sponsored by the Aladdin Lamp Company, as a result of which they were renamed the Aladdin Laddies! Then came a similar gig from the makers of Light Crust Flour, and they became the Light Crust Doughboys. This was where Wills developed the jazz element which would be the trademark of Western Swing, which he brought to fruition with the addition a second fiddler, pedal steel guitar, trumpet, trombone, saxophone and clarinet in the Texas Playboys.

Profile: Bob Wills (fiddle)
Born: James Robert Wills, 6 March 1905, Kosse, Texas
Died: 13 May 1975, Fort Worth, Texas

Recording Debut: November, 1929 (duo with guitarist Herman Arnspiger)

Classic Records: San Antonio Rose; We Might As Well Forget It; You're From Texas; Smoke On The Water; New San Antonio Rose; Take Me Back To Tulsa

Facts'n'Figures: As success followed success, the Playboys got bigger and bigger – literally. Their 1939 hit 'San Antonio Rose' (which Wills had written in '36) was remade the following year as 'New San Antonio Rose' with an 18-piece band that included two trumpets and a five-strong reed section. It sold over a million copies, became the Playboys' signature tune, and was also a huge pop hit for Bing Crosby in 1941. The largest line-up of all came in 1944 when the band numbered 21 musicians.

Evident in the work of musicians like Freddie Slack and Bill Haley, Western Swing also became one of the early ingredients in the musical melting pot that produced the first rock'n'roll. With vocalist Ella Mae Morse, pianist Slack had a huge hit in 1946 with the boogie-based "House Of Blue Lights", an early harbinger of rock if ever there was one. And in the early Fifties Bill Haley led the Four Aces of Western Swing, the Down Homers and the Saddlemen – the latter changing their name to the Comets before having the first-ever rock'n'roll entry in the Top Ten with 'Shake Rattle And Roll' in 1954.

There was a revival of interest in Western Swing in the Seventies, with a Bob Wills tribute album *The Last Time* being organised by Merle Haggard, and Waylon Jennings writing 'Bob Wills Is Still The King', a Number One country hit in 1975. The sound was also influential on a number of country rock bands including Commander Cody and his Lost Planet Airmen, and a direct inspiration for Riders In the Sky, Asleep At The Wheel (the finest revivalist Western Swing group of them all) and the Hot Club of Cowtown, who still operate out of their home base of Dallas.

"I can't think of a country artist we ever listened to and learned their tunes. We listened to Benny Goodman, Glenn Miller, Louis Armstrong..."
Bob Wills' pedal steel player Leon McAuliffe

GOOD TIMIN'

HONKY TONK

Originally a term used to describe the kind of 'speakeasy' music joints that served illegal alcohol during the years of Prohibition, by the Forties "honky tonk" had come to refer to the first truly urban form of country music.

After the Depression of the Thirties, millions of rural Americans moved to the cities in search of work, spurred first by the industrialisation of Theodore Roosevelt's New Deal programme of urban regeneration, then the added impetus of defence jobs at the onset of World War II.

Like Western Swing before it, honky tonk music originated out of Texas. The oil boom there that preceded America's industrial recovery had seen an upsurge in dance halls and nightclubs, and a new brand of country followed the hillbilly swing outfits in filling these venues.

Honky tonk saw the introduction of electric instruments to country music proper, again following the example of Bob Wills and other Western Swing outfits. One of honky tonk's pioneers, Ernest Tubb, is credited as being the first country artist to employ an electric guitar in his line-up, when he recorded 'Walkin' The Floor Over You' with guitarist Fay "Smitty" Smith in 1941.

Other early honky tonk heroes included Roy Acuff, "Lefty" Frizzell, Al Dexter (whose 'Honky Tonk Blues' was the first song to have the phrase in its title) and Floyd Tillman – but the biggest star of all to come out of honky tonk music was the legendary Hank Williams.

EARLY HONKY TONK HITS

Al Dexter
Honky Tonk Blues[1937]
Ernest Tubb
Walkin' The Floor Over You[1941]
Roy Acuff
I'll Forgive You But I Can't Forget[1944]
Red Foley
Smoke On The Water[1944]
Floyd Tillman
They Took The Stars Out Of Heaven[1949]
Lefty Frizell
If You've Got The Money, I've Got The Time [1950]

In 1943 Al Dexter's 'Pistol Packin' Mama' was the first million-selling Number One on both the US country and pop charts. An out-and-out pop version by Bing

Crosby and the Andrews Sisters also sold a million, and the song later proved a rockabilly-style hit for Gene Vincent in 1960.

Hank Williams was certainly the biggest star to emerge with honky tonk, and arguably the most famous name in country music history. From his debut on the *Grand Ole Opry* in 1949 to his untimely death (brought on by an addiction to pills and drink) on New Year's Day 1953, he sold millions of records, and for posterity wrote some of the all-time classic standards of country music.

Profile: Hank Williams (vocals, guitar)
Born: Hiram Williams, 17 September 1923, Butler County, Alabama
Died: 1 January 1953, Oak Hill, West Virginia

Recording Debut: 11 December 1946, 'Callin' You'/ 'When God Comes And Gathers His Jewels' (for the Sterling label in Nashville)

Classic Records: Honky Tonkin'; Lovesick Blues; Lost Highway; I'm So Lonesome I Could Cry; Long Gone Lonesome Blues; Why Don't You Love Me?; Moanin' The Blues; You Win Again; Cold, Cold Heart; Hey Good Lookin'; Jambalaya; Kaw-Liga; Your Cheatin' Heart; Take These Chains From My Heart.

Facts'n'Figures: Between 1949 and 1953, Hank Williams had no less than twelve records make the top of the US country charts. 'Lovesick Blues' topped the list in '49, followed by 'I'm So Lonesome I Could Cry', with 'Long Gone Lonesome Blues', 'Why Don't

You Love Me?' and 'Moanin' The Blues' topping the chart in 1950. In 1951 'Cold, Cold Heart' and 'Hey Good Lookin'' made the pole position, as did 'Jambalaya' and 'I'll Never Get Out Of This World Alive' in '52. And immediately after his death he had three postumous Number Ones in 1953, 'Kaw-Liga', 'Your Cheatin' Heart' and 'Take These Chains From My Heart'. In addition, six sides reached the Number Two spot during the same period.

On January 1, 1953, Hank Williams was due to play in Canton, Ohio, but his flight was cancelled due to bad weather. He hired a chauffeur and, before leaving the Andrew Johnson Hotel in Knoxville, Tennessee, was injected with B12 and morphine. He then left in a Cadillac, clutching a bottle of whiskey. When Charles Carr, the seventeen-year-old driver, pulled over at an all-night gas station in Oak Hill, West Virginia, he discovered that Williams was unresponsive. Closer examination revealed that Hank Williams was, in fact, dead.

Honky tonk stars who followed in the wake of Hank Williams included Webb Pierce who hit with 'More And More' [1954] and 'Teenage Boogie' [1956], Ray Price with 'Don't Let The Stars Get Into Your Eyes' [1952], 'Crazy Arms' [1956], and 'City Lights' [1958], and Johnny Horton with 'Honky Tonk Man' in 1956.

ROCKABILLY

When honky tonk country music fused with black rhythm and blues to produce the earliest rock'n'roll, one of the most potent results of that mix came to be known as rockabilly ("rock and hillbilly").

With its emphasis on amplified guitars, voices recorded with lots of echo and a slapped double bass, the characteristic sound of rockabilly was developed in America's South by pioneering record labels, the most influential of which was Sun Records in Memphis. The "Sun sound" was created by producer Sam Phillips, with a clutch of early rock'n'rollers that included Carl Perkins, Warren Smith, Billy Riley, Sonny Burgess, Jerry Lee Lewis, Roy Orbison, the young Johnny Cash and, most famously of all, the teenage Elvis Presley.

The first ever true rockabilly record is generally considered to have been Elvis' first single, recorded at Sun in early July 1954 and released later that month. The A-side was 'That's All Right', written and first recorded by Arthur "Big Boy" Crudup, on which Elvis delivered a blues number with a country feel; the flip-side was 'Blue Moon Of Kentucky' by Bill Monroe, where conversely a bluegrass standard was done with a blues feel.

Credited on the label simply as "Elvis, Scotty and Bill", the single featured Elvis on guitar and vocals, guitarist Scotty Moore and Bill Black on bass. By the middle of August 'Blue Moon Of Kentucky' had reached the Number 3 spot on *Billboard*'s regional Country and Western chart for the Memphis area, and at the end of the month entered the Country and Western chart for the whole Mid-South region. Rather than the rhythm and blues-slanted A-side, it was the country-tinged B-side that first put Elvis on the map – he even toured the Southern states billed as "The Hillbilly Cat."

The actual term "rockabilly" was first coined by Bill Flagg, describing his 1956 hit 'Go Cat Go' and its 1957 follow-up 'Guitar Rock.' The phrase soon caught on, and first caught the ears of mainstream music fans in 1957 when pop singer Guy Mitchell's single 'Rock-A-Billy' made the US Top Ten, and topped the charts in the UK – although, save for the title, the record bore little resemblance to actual rockabilly.

Rockabilly forged a cross-over point between country music and straight commercial pop, as can be heard in the records of artists as diverse as Gene Vincent, Ricky Nelson, Eddie Cochran, Buddy Holly and the Everly Brothers. Holly and the Everlys were subsequently a particular influence on the music of the Beatles, who also acknowledged rockabilly when they recorded three Carl Perkins numbers in 1964 – 'Matchbox', 'Everybody's Trying To Be My Baby' and 'Honey Don't.'

RED HOT ROCKABILLIES

Ten classics from the golden age
of rockabilly

Artist / Title / US Label / Year

Elvis Presley *Baby Let's Play House*
Sun 1955

Eddie Fontaine *Cool It Baby*
Decca 1956

Johnny Burnette *Honey Hush*
Coral 1957

Jerry Lee Lewis *Whole Lotta Shakin Goin' On*
Sun 1957

Eddie Cochran *Twenty Flight Rock*
Liberty 1957

Buddy Holly *Rock Around With Ollie Vee*
Decca 1957

Marvin Rainwater *My Brand Of Blues*
MGM 1957

Peanuts Wilson *Cast Iron Arm*
Brunswick 1957

Carl Perkins *Matchbox*
Sun 1957

Wanda Jackson *Fujiyama Mama*
Capitol 1958

COUNTRY MUSIC ASSOCIATION
AWARD WINNERS
1967-2005

Year	Entertainer of the Year	Male Vocalist	Female Vocalist
1967	Eddy Arnold	Jack Greene	Loretta Lynn
1968	Glen Campbell	Glen Campbell	Tammy Wynette
1969	Johnny Cash	Johnny Cash	Tammy Wynette
1970	Merle Haggard	Merle Haggard	Tammy Wynette
1971	Charley Pride	Charley Pride	Lynn Anderson
1972	Loretta Lynn	Charley Pride	Loretta Lynn
1973	Roy Clark	Charlie Rich	Loretta Lynn
1974	Charlie Rich	Ronnie Milsap	Olivia Newton-John
1975	John Denver	Waylon Jennings	Dolly Parton
1976	Mel Tillis	Ronnie Milsap	Dolly Parton
1977	Ronnie Milsap	Ronnie Milsap	Crystal Gayle
1978	Dolly Parton	Don Williams	Crystal Gayle
1979	Willie Nelson	Kenny Rogers	Barbara Mandrell
1980	Barbara Mandrell	George Jones	Emmylou Harris
1981	Barbara Mandrell	George Jones	Barbara Mandrell
1982	Alabama	Ricky Scaggs	Janie Fricke
1983	Alabama	Lee Greenwood	Janie Fricke
1984	Alabama	Lee Greenwood	Reba McEntire

1985	Ricky Skaggs	George Strait	Reba McEntire
1986	Reba McEntire	George Strait	Reba McEntire
1987	Hank Williams, Jr.	Randy Travis	Reba McEntire
1988	Hank Williams Jr.	Randy Travis	K.T. Oslin
1989	George Strait	Ricky Van Shelton	Kathy Mattea
1990	George Strait	Clint Black	Kathy Mattea
1991	Garth Brooks	Vince Gill	Tanya Tucker
1992	Garth Brooks	Vince Gill	Mary Chapin Carpenter
1993	Vince Gill	Vince Gill	Mary Chapin Carpenter
1994	Vince Gill	Vince Gill	Pam Tillis
1995	Alan Jackson	Vince Gill	Alison Krauss
1996	Brooks & Dunn	George Strait	Patty Loveless
1997	Garth Brooks	George Strait	Trisha Yearwood
1998	Garth Brooks	George Strait	Trisha Yearwood
1999	Shania Twain	Tim Mcgraw	Martina McBride
2000	Dixie Chicks	Tim Mcgraw	Faith Hill
2001	Tim McGraw	Toby Keith	Lee Ann Womack
2002	Alan Jackson	Alan Jackson	Martina McBride
2003	Alan Jackson	Alan Jackson	Martina McBride
2004	Kenney Chesney	Keith Urban	Martina McBride
2005	Keith Urban	Keith Urban	Gretchen Wilson

THE NASHVILLE ERA

Nashville's ascending importance as a centre of country music began after World War II with the growing popularity of the *Grand Ole Opry* based in the city. Several recording studios opened up there, leading to an influx of musicians.

It also reflected an increasing crossover of country material into the pop mainstream, an early instance of which was when Patti Page (best remembered for 1953's 'How Much Is That Doggy on The Window') sold more than three million copies of 'Tennessee Waltz' in 1950, penned by country writers Pee Wee King and Redd Stewart in 1947. And country music's greatest composer, Hank Williams, as well as gracing the pop charts himself many times, saw his songs covered successfully by the likes of Tony Bennett with the chart-topping 'Cold Cold Heart' in 1951, and Jo Stafford's Top Ten duet with Frankie Laine on 'Hey Good Lookin'' the same year.

The American composers' copyright organisation BMI (Broadcasting Music Industries) began to exert an active influence in Nashville in the early Fifties, in

1953 starting the annual Country Awards. And in 1954 the "Country Music Disc Jockey's Association" – later to become the CMA (Country Music Association) in 1958 – was created, by which time there were reckoned to be as many songwriters in Nashville as in New York. In 1961 the CMA founded the Country Music Hall of Fame, and in 1967 held the first annual CMA Awards ceremony – now the biggest annual awards event in country music.

The CMA Awards ceremony attracts nearly 40 million television viewers in the USA and is broadcast live to radio stations in Australia, Germany, Ireland, Luxembourg, the Netherlands and the UK.

MUSIC SQUARE

The ever-expanding Music Row district came to include the development of Music Square, where literally dozens of publishers, record companies and studios are now located, including the multi-nationals listed here.

Sony Music Publishing	8 Music Square West
RCA Studio B	30 Music Square West
United Artists Tower	50 Music Square West
MCA Records	60 Music Square East
Mercury Records	54 Music Square East
EMI Music Publishing	35 Music Square East
Sony Music	34 Music Square East
Warner Chappell Music	21 Music Square East

By the early Sixties Music Row – located on Sixteenth Avenue South in downtown Nashville – was the site of a multitude of publishing and record company offices and recording studios. The city became known as "Music City USA", and by 1963 one out of every two records produced in America came out of a Nashville studio.

THE NASHVILLE SOUND

The classic "Nashville sound" of the Fifties and Sixties was basically country music played with a pop frame of mind. There was an increasing emphasis on guitar and piano in place of the fiddle, steel guitar and other traditional instruments, and records often featured overtly "commercial" trappings such as backing vocal choruses and string orchestras.

The prime architect of the Nashville sound was Chet Atkins, a virtuoso guitarist who adapted the finger-picking style of his mentor Merle Travis. By applying a banjo technique, Travis made the guitar a rhythmic and melodic instrument simulataneously, and Atkins simplified Travis' style by using three "picking" fingers instead of two.

Atkins had also been working on the production side for RCA since 1952, and was appointed to run its new Nashville studio in 1957, and it was in that context that he helped create the archetypal Nashville style of record.

Profile: Chet Atkins (guitar)
Born: Chester Burton Atkins, 20 June 1924,
Luttrell, Tennessee
Died: 30 June 2001, Nashville, Tennessee

Recording Debut: 1946 for Bullet label, signing to
RCA '47

Classic Records: 'Mr Sandman', 'Canned Heat',
'Chinatown, My Chinatown', 'Country Gentleman',
'Downhill Drag' plus many albums including *Gallopin'
Guitar, Finger Style Guitar, Mister Guitar, Teensville* and
Chet Atkins Workshop

Facts'n'Figures: Chet Atkins received 14 Grammys,
9 CMA "Instrumentalist of the Year" awards, 19
consecutive *Cashbox* awards and 4 *Playboy* Jazz Poll
honours. Plus a "Lifetime Achievement Award" from
the National Academy of Recording Arts & Sciences
(NARAS)

Chet Atkins helped coordinate the legendary session at
the original Nashville RCA studios on January 10
1956, which produced Elvis Presley's first recordings
for the label – including his first chart-topper
'Heartbreak Hotel'. Atkins played guitar on the session
too.

> *"...Everyone has their own sound, and if you're heard enough,
> folks will come to recognize it. Style however, is a different thing.
> Try to express your own ideas. It's much more difficult to do, but the
> rewards are there if you're good enough to pull it off..."*
> Chet Atkins

COUNTRY-POP CROSSOVERS

Ten Top Ten hits that came in the wake of
the Nashville sound

Year / Artist / Title / US Pop Chart

1957 Marty Robbins
A White Sport Coat #2

1957 Ferlin Husky
Gone #4

1958 Conway Twitty
It's Only Make Believe #1

1958 Don Gibson
Oh Lonesome Me #7

1959 Marty Robbins
El Paso #1

1960 Jim Reeves
He'll Have to Go #2

1961 Leroy Van Dyke
Walk On By #5

1961 Jimmy Dean
Big Bad John #1

1965 Roger Miller
King of the Road #4

1965 Eddy Arnold
Make The World Go Away #6

HONKY TONK ANGELS

There had been highly successful female country singers since Patsy Montana sold a million with 'I Wanna Be A Cowboy's Sweetheart' in 1935. But the country girls really came into their own in the Nashville era, with names like Patsy Cline, Brenda Lee and Tammy Wynette all becoming household names.

LEADING LADIES OF THE NASHVILLE ERA

ARTIST	BIGGEST HIT	YEAR	US CHART
Brenda Lee	I'm Sorry	1960	#1
Patsy Cline	Crazy	1961	#9
Skeeter Davis	The End Of the World	1963	#2
Tammy Wynette	Stand By Your Man	1968	#19
Jeannie C Riley	Harper Valley PTA	1968	#1

The big breakthrough for country gals came via Kitty Wells with a record written by Jay Miller. 'It Wasn't God Who Made Honky Tonk Angels' was a 1952 "answer record" to Hank Thompson's hugely success-ful 'Wild Side Of Life' which included the line "I didn't know God made honky tonk angels". Kitty's disc was a surprise smash, and opened the door for female country vocalists, often singing songs that expressed a woman's point of view.

COUNTRY LADIES' CLASSICS

Songs from a feminin' point of view

Hot Dog! That Made Him Mad
Wanda Jackson 1956

Second Fiddle (To An Old Guitar)
Jean Shepard 1964

*Don't Come Home A-Drinking
(With Loving On Your Mind)*
Loretta Lynn 1966

I Never Promised You A Rose Garden
Lyn Anderson 1970

Nine To Five
Dolly Parton 1981

You're The First Time I've Thought About Leaving
Reba McEntire 1983

Take It Like A Man
Michelle Wright 1992

A Woman Knows
Martina McBride 1992

You Never Will
Suzy Bogguss 1993

What Part Of No
Lorrie Morgan 2002

One of the biggest boosts to the mainstream popularity of country music during the Nashville era came in the unlikely person of rhythm and blues and soul singer Ray Charles, whose 1962 album *Modern Sounds In Country And Western Music* topped the album charts. It sold over half a million copies in its first two months of release, with the first single to be taken from it – a cover of Don Gibson's 'I Can't Stop Loving You' – topping the singles charts.

THE FIRST QUEEN OF COUNTRY

One of the first female singers to make it big in the previously male-dominated world of country music was **Patsy Cline**. With an emotionally powerful voice, her melodic records with their silky arrangements were the epitome of the Nashville sound.

Profile: Patsy Cline (vocals)
Born: Virginia Petterson Hensley, 8 September 1932, Winchester Virginia
Died: 5 March 1963, Camden, Tennessee

Recording Debut: 1954 for the Four Star label

Classic Records: 'Walkin' After Midnight', I Fall To Pieces', 'Crazy', 'She's Got You', 'When I Get Thru With You', 'Heartaches', 'Sweet Dreams', Faded Love'

Facts'n'Figures: Between 1957 and her untimely death in 1963, Patsy Cline had eight entries in the Country & Western Top Ten, including two Number Ones, and in the same period had five records in the Top Twenty pop charts.

Nearly twenty years after her death in a plane crash that also claimed the lives of country stars Cowboy Copas, Hawkshaw Hawkins and Randy Hughes, Patsy Cline was featured on two macabre "duet" hits in 1981. Her voice was dubbed alongside that of Jim Reeves, who similarly died in an air fatality in 1964, a year after Cline, on 'Have You Ever Been Lonely' and 'I Fall To Pieces'.

Covering Cline
Alternate versions of songs made famous
by Patsy Cline

Crazy
covered by: Slim Dusty
Willie Nelson, Ray Price, Kenny Rogers,
Linda Ronstadt

I Fall To Pieces
covered by: Ralph McTell, Michael Nesmith,
Linda Ronstadt

Sweet Dreams
covered by: Elvis Costello, Don Everly,
Emmylou Harris, Reba McEntire

She's Got You
covered by: Lee Ann Womack, Loretta Lynn,
LeAnn Rimes

Walkin' After Midnight
covered by: Garth Brooks,
Bryan Adams, Loretta Lynn

Faded Love
covered by: George Jones, Elvis Presley,
LeAnn Rimes

FROM THE BACKWOODS TO DOLLYWOOD

The most celebrated female country star of the last thirty years has undoubtedly been Dolly Parton. Her over-the-top image has often belied her achievements as a highly accomplished singer and musician, a memorable songwriter and astute business woman.

Dolly Parton has often referred to her humble beginnings in the backwoods of Tennessee mountain country in such songs as 'Coat Of Many Colors' and 'My Tennessee Mountain Home'. Apparently her parents were so poor that when she was born – the fourth in a family of twelve children – the doctor attending the birth had to be paid in corn meal.

 Profile: Dolly Parton (vocals, guitar, banjo etc)
Born: Dolly Rebecca Parton, 19 January 1946, Locust Ridge, Sevier County, Tennessee

Recording Debut: 'Puppy Love' for the small Louisian label Gold Band label, recorded in 1957 when Dolly was eleven years old, and released in April 1959.

Classic Records: 'Last Thing On My Mind', 'We'll Get Ahead Some Day', 'Tomorrow Is Forever', 'Daddy Was An Old-Time Preacher Man' (all with Porter Waggoner). 'Mule Skinner Blues', 'Joshua', 'Coat of Many Colors', 'Touch Your Woman', 'My Tennessee Mountain Home', 'Jolene', 'I Will Always Love You',

'Love Is Like A Butterfly', 'The Bargain Store', 'Here You Come Again', '9 to 5', 'Shine'. Albums include *Joshua*, *Coat of Many Colors*, *The Grass Is Blue*, and *Trio* and *Trio II*, both with Linda Ronstadt and Emmylou Harris

Facts'n'Figures: With over 40 nominations since 1969, Dolly Parton has won seven Grammy Awards: Best Country Vocal Performance in 1978 for *Here You Come Again*, and in 1981 for '9 to 5'; Best Country Song in 1981 for '9 to 5'; Best Country Performance By A Duo Or Group With Vocal in 1987 for *Trio* with Emmylou Harris and Linda Ronstadt; Best Country Vocal Collaboration with Emmylou Harris and Linda Ronstadt for 'After The Goldrush' in 2000; Best Bluegrass Album in 2001 for *The Grass Is Blue* and Best Female Country Vocal Performance in 2002 for 'Shine'.

As well as her recording triumphs over the years, in the country and mainstream popcharts, Dolly Parton has featured in innumerable TV music shows and in an acting role in several sitcoms. She has also appeared in Hollywood movies, the most notable of which have been *Nine to Five* [1980], *The Best Little Whorehouse in Texas* in 1982, and 1989's *Steel Magnolia*s. Much of her vast earnings from these various activities – plus touring, but only when she chooses to – have been ploughed into her highly successful Dollywood theme park in her native Tennessee.

"If I hadn't been a woman,
I'd have been a drag queen"
Dolly Parton

KEEP ON TRUCKIN'

Trucker songs are a tough high-octane sub-genre of country music which first made itself felt as early as Ted Daffen's 'Truck Driver's Blues' in 1938, and have continued to cruise the country charts ever since. They enjoyed something of a boom in the Seventies with the craze for CB (citizen's band) radio, with "CB" hits like Dave Dudley's 'Me and Ole C.B.', Red Sovine's tearjerker 'Teddy Bear' and C.W. McCall's chart-topping 'Convoy'.

TWELVE TOP TRUCKER SONGS

Year / Artist / Title / Country Chart

1963 Dave Dudley
Six Days On the Road #2 (pop #32)

1970 Dick Curless
Big Wheel Cannonball #27

1971 Red Simpson
I'm a Truck #4

1973 Dave Dudley
Keep On Truckin' #19

1975 Dave Dudley
Me and Ole C.B. #12

1975 C.W. McCall
Convoy #1 (pop #1)

1975 Merle Haggard
Movin' On #1

1976 Cledus Maggard
The White Knight #1 (pop #19)

1976 Red Sovine
Teddy Bear #1 (pop #40)

1981 Razzy Bailey
Midnight Hauler #1

1984 Alabama
Roll On (Eighteen Wheeler) #1

1988 Kathy Mattea
Eighteen Wheels and a Dozen Roses #1

THE MAN IN BLACK

In a career that spanned five decades, from his rockabilly days with Sun Records in the mid-Fifties until his
death in 2003, Johnny Cash was one of the great icons
of country music.

His first backing group, billed as The Tennessee Two,
consisted of Luther Perkins on guitar and Marshall
Grant on bass. When they first auditioned for Sun
Records in Memphis, singing just gospel songs, producer Sam Phillips told Cash to "go home and sin,
then come back with a song I can sell".

*"Sam Phillips always encouraged me to do it my way, to use
what ever other influences I wanted, but never to copy... that was a
great rare gift he gave me: believe in myself, right from the start
of my recording career... if there hadn't been a Sam Phillips,
I might still be working in a cotton field"*
Johnny Cash

Profile: Johnny Cash (vocals, guitar)
Born: John Ray Cash, 26 February 1932,
Kingsland, Arkansas
Died: 12 September 2003, Nashville, Tennessee

Recording Debut: 'Hey Porter' / 'Cry, Cry, Cry',
released on Sun Records in June 1955 as Johnny Cash
And The Tennessee Two, reached #14 on the US country charts.

Classic Records: 'I Walk The Line', 'Ballad Of A
Teenage Queen', 'Guess Things Happen That Way',
'The Ways Of A Woman In Love', 'Don't Take Your
Guns To Town', 'Ring Of Fire', 'A Boy Name Sue',
'Jackson' (with June Carter), 'If I Were A Carpenter'
(with June Carter). Albums include *Johnny Cash At
Fulsom Prison, Johnny Cash At San Quentin Prison, The
Man In Black, Highwayman* (with Kris Kristofferson,
Waylon Jennings and Willie Nelson), *American
Recordings, Unchained.*

Facts'n'Figures: In 1969 Cash swept the Country
Music Association (CMA) Awards with his San
Quentin live album and the single taken from it 'A Boy
Named Sue'. As well as his being named Entertainer of
the Year and Male Vocalist of the Year, 'Sue' was
honoured as Single of the Year while Johnny Cash At
San Quentin received the Album of the Year accolade.

One of Johnny Cash's more unusual awards among his
thirteen Grammys was for Best Album Notes in 1969,
for the poem 'Of Bob Dylan' which he wrote for the
back cover of Bob Dylan's Nashville Skyline. On the
album Dylan and Cash duetted on a new version of
Dylan's 1963 classic 'Girl From The North Country'.

"Johnny Cash has only passed into the greater light. He will only become more important in this industry as time goes by... "
Dolly Parton

RHINESTONE COWBOYS ...AND COWGIRLS

The "rhinestone cowboy" look beloved of country and western performers has its roots early in the 20th century when rodeo stars began to dress up in outfits designed to catch the eye, with bright colours and flamboyant embroidery and trimmings adorning practical riding clothes.

Rodeo Ben of Philadelphia was the earliest of the famous cowboy couturiers, after his creations made in the Twenties for rodeo and circus folk attracted the attention of Hollywood western stars like Tom Mix – and later the "singing cowboys" including Gene Autry and Roy Rogers.

When Nathan Turk opened his Western and English Apparel shop in Los Angeles in the Forties, his musical customers included Ernest Tubb, Spade Cooley and western swing bandleader Hank Thompson. Turk, who was actually a Polish immigrant called Nathan Tieg, drew on the colourfully embroidered folk dress of Eastern Europe for much of his inspiration – one of his prime sources was a book called National Costumes of Austria, Hungary, Poland and Czechoslovakia.

Most celebrated of all was the Ukranian-born Brooklyn tailor Nutya Kotlyrenko, better known as Nudie Cohn or just simply Nudie. He moved to the west coast after creating lavish costumes for exotic dancers in New York strip clubs, and when he opened his Hollywood shop in 1947 his clothes were an immediate hit with cowboy movie stars and hillbilly singers alike.

Among his most famous creations was the 24-carat gold lamé suit worn by Elvis Presley.

Country singers dressed by Nudie included Hank Williams, Left Frizell, Little Jimmy Dickens, Ernest Tubb, Kitty Wells, Webb Pierce, Pee Wee King, Porter Wagoner, Hank Snow, Buck Owens, Tammy Wynette, Merle Haggard and George Jones.

Nudie died in 1984, and one of his top designers Manuel (Manuel Cuevas) set up his own business in Nashville, dressing (among many others) country stars Alan Jackson, Travis Tritt and Dwight Yoakam. Dolly Parton, Linda Ronstadt and Emmylou Harris commissioned Manuel to design their outfits used on the cover of their 1987 album Trio.

THE BAKERSFIELD SOUND

The Bakersfield Sound was an early Sixties West Coast alternative to the increasingly slick music coming out of Nashville, originating in and around Bakersfield, California.

With an economy based on agriculture and oil, the town became a magnet for migrants during the Depression – the "Okies" from Oklahoma plus workers from all over Texas, Arkansas and other parts of the southwest. They brought their music with them, and one of the first groups to make it big on the West Coast was the Maddox Brothers and Rose who had a string of country hits through the Thirties and Forties.

A hard-edged reaction to the boom in Nashville-style country music, the Bakersfield "sound" utilised electric instrumentation and a pronounced backbeat borrowed from rockabilly, together with elements of traditional country music and Western Swing. It was forged by artsists such as Buck Owens, Merle Haggard and Tommy Collins, and soon made its mark in the mainstream market.

The legacy of Bakersfield country can be heard in the work of later musicians and singers, notably in the work of Dwight Yoakam. It was also a huge influence on the country pioneer Gram Parsons.

BAKERSFIELD BIGGIES

Year	Artist	Title	US Country Chart
1959	Buck Owens	Under Your Spell Again	#4
1966	Merle Haggard	Okie From Muskogee	#9
1967	Wynn Stewart	It's Such A Pretty World Today	#1
1971	Red Simpson	I'm a Truck	#4
1988	Dwight Yoakam	The Streets of Bakersfield [withBuck Owens]	#1

Maverick Country

OUTLAW MUSIC

Stylistically closely related to the Bakersfield sound, and similarly a reaction to the seeming blandness of much of the music coming out of Nashville, 'outlaw country' was a significant trend in the late Sixties and through the Seventies featuring tough music that took no prisoners.

Although Nashville continued to be the commercial centre of country, many felt the music's soul was better represented in places like Bakersfield, California, and Austin and Lubbock, both in Texas. The Texas connection was central to the outlaw movement, which sought to bring back to country the rawness and authenticity of pioneers like Jimmy Rodgers, Hank Williams and Lefty Frizell.

The term 'outlaw country' came from the song 'Ladies Love Outlaws' written by Lee Clayton and sung by Waylon Jennings on the 1972 album of the same name. Jennings was a leading voice in the outlaw movement, alongside names such as Willie Nelson, Johnny Cash,

Merle Haggard, David Allan Coe and Kris Kristofferson. He took the genre into the Top Ten album charts in 1976 with *The Outlaws*, which also featured Willie Nelson, Jessi Colter and Tompall Glaser.

> *"I've always felt that blues, rock'n'roll and country are just about a beat apart."*
> Waylon Jennings

Profile: Willie Nelson

Born: Willie Hugh Nelson, 30 April 1933, Abbot, Texas

Recording Debut: 'No Place For Me'/'Lumberjack' recorded in Vancouver, Washington in 1956. He sold it over the air via a local radio show on which he was DJ – $1 for the disc and a signed photo.

Classic Records: 'Touch Me', 'I Never Cared For You', 'My Own Peculiar Way', 'Laying My Burdens Down', 'Whiskey River', 'Bubbles In My Beer', 'Blue Eyes Crying In The Rain', 'Mammas Don't Let Your Babies Grow Up To Be Cowboys' (with Waylon Jennings), 'Georgia On My Mind', 'All Of Me'. Albums: *Yesterday's Wine, Shotgun Willie, Phases And Stages, Red Headed Stranger, Waylon and Willie* (with Waylon Jennings), *Stardust, One For The Road* (with Leon Russell), *San Antonio Rose* (with Ray Price), *Pancho And Lefty* (with Merle Haggard), *Who'll Buy My Memories, Across The Borderline, Just One Love, It Always Will Be, Countryman*

Facts'n'Figures: As well as his many hit singles and albums, Willie Nelson initially enjoyed greater success as a songwriter. Hits of his compositions by other artists include 1961's 'Crazy' by Patsy Cline, Claude Gray with the 1960 hit 'Family Bible', Faron Young's 'Hello Walls' in 1961, 'Night Life' by Ray Price, and 'Funny How Time Slips Away', a 1961 hit for both country star Billy Walker and pop singer Jimmy Elledge.

Drawing on honky-tonk, the Bakersfield sound and country rock, outlaw music had a distinctly hard edge to it and, importantly, appealed to a post-Vietnam audience that had previously considered country music the preserve of rednecks.

THE HIGHWAYMEN

A crucial album of the outlaw style came in 1985 with the eponymous *The Highwaymen*, another name for the 'supergroup' line-up of Johnny Cash, Waylon Jennings, Willie Nelson and Kris Kristofferson. Scoring a #1 country hit with the single 'Highwayman' from the album, the group also topped the country album chart. They got together again in 1990 for a sequel, *Highwaymen 2*, which got to #4 on the country album charts and spun off a minor hit 'Silver Stallion'. And in 1995 the foursome reconvened yet again for *The Road Goes On Forever*.

Other landmark 'outlaw' records included the Jennings and Nelson collaboration *Waylon & Willie*, which made #12 in the US pop charts in 1978, and the teaming of Merle Haggard and Willie Nelson for the memorable *Poncho & Lefty* in 1983.

··········· COUNTRY ROCK ···········

Although they were more associated with the main-stream rock'n'roll of the Fifties and early Sixties, the first manifestation of what could be termed country rock was in the work of the Everly Brothers. They brought the close harmonies and melodic tradition of country into the rock arena with hits like 'Bye Bye Love', 'When Will I Be Loved' and 'Wake Up Little Susie', many of which were written by country song-writing giants Felice and Boudleaux Bryant.

Highly influenced by the Bakersfield sound, guitarist and singer Gram Parsons was a pioneering figure in what became labelled as country rock. The label was almost inevitable. Just as Bob Dylan had moved from out-and-out folk music when he came under the spell of the Beatles and the other British beat groups, to forge an electric-fusion that the press named 'folk rock', so Dylan-accolites The Byrds – when they briefly included Gram Parsons – took it one step further, Parsons soon leaving to form the Flying Burrito Brothers to move things into an even more country-tinged direction.

This was at a time when, to the youth of America in the grip of firstly Beatlemania, then psychedelia (with Dylan's protest/folk rock thrown in for good measure), Nashville-style country music was decidedly uncool. Two important events were to change this. First of all The Byrds, who'd had chart hits like 'Mr Tambourine Man' and 'Eight Miles High', became the first rock band to play the Grand Ole Opry, releasing in 1968 the seminal *Sweetheart of the Rodeo* which became a template for country rock to come. Then, in 1969, Bob Dylan was to release *Nashville Skyline*, on which he duetted with Johnny Cash to the amazement of the rock fans, to whom any whiff of country had previously been anathema. And also in 1969 the Flying Burrito Brothers, with Gram Parsons, released what is considered the first country rock album proper, *Gilded Palace of Sin*.

COUNTRY ROCK CLASSICS

Year / Artist / Title / US Pop chart

1968
The Byrds *Sweetheart Of The Rodeo*
1969
Bob Dylan *Nashville Skyline* #3
1969
The Band *The Band* #9
1969
Flying Burrito Brothers *Gilded Palace of Sin*
1976
Emmylou Harris *Elite Hotel* #23

THE QUEEN OF COUNTRY ROCK

With the death of Gram Parsons in 1973, country rock found a new star in Linda Ronstadt whose backing group went on to enjoy, as the Eagles, huge success as a country-influenced rock band in the Seventies. Other big names in country rock during that era included

Charlie Daniels, Doctor Hook and the Medicine Show, Poco, The Nitty Gritty Dirt Band and Gram Parsons' one-time singing partner who became regarded as the 'queen' of country rock, Emmylou Harris.

 Profile: Emmylou Harris
Born: 12 April, 1949, Birmingham, Alabama

Recording Debut: 1970 album *Gliding Bird* for the small independent Jubilee label.

Classic Records: 'Wheels of Love', 'If I Could Only Win Your Love', 'You Never Can Tell', 'Never Be Anyone', 'High Powered Love', 'To Know Him Is To Love Him' and 'High Sierra' (both with Dolly Parton and Linda Ronstadt), 'A Love That Will Never Grow Old'. Albums: *Pieces of the Sky*, *Elite Hotel*, *Luxury Liner*, *Quarter Moon In A Ten Cent Town*, *Roses In The Snow*, *The Ballad Of Sally Rose*, *Evangeline*, *Trio* and *Trio II* (both with Dolly Parton and Linda Ronstadt)

Facts'n'Figures: Since 1998, Emmylou Harris has organized an annual benefit tour called Concerts for a Landmine Free World. All proceeds support the Vietnam Veterans of America Foundation's (VVAF) efforts to assist innocent victims of conflicts around the world. Artists that have joined Harris on the road for these benefits have included Mary-Chapin Carpenter, Bruce Cockburn, Steve Earle, Joan Baez, Patty Griffin John Prine, Elvis Costello and Nanci Griffith.

For over 15 years Emmylou fronted the aptly-named Hot Band, whose various line-ups included such prestigious players as Elvis' Las Vegas guitar man James Burton, UK ace guitarist Albert Lee, ex-Crickets Glen D.Hardin on piano, bass player Emory Gordy Jnr, and then-unknown Rodney Crowell (guitar) and Ricky Scaggs (fiddle and mandolin), later both big names in their own right.

While the 'outlaw' bands deliberately 'dressed down' in rough-looking jeans, workshirts and basic stetson hats as part of their reaction against Nashville glitter and glitz, the country rock acts – particularly Gram Parsons and Emmylou Harris – often appeared in Nudie-style embrodered finery in homage to the music that until then had been rejected by rock audiences.

PROGRESSIVE COUNTRY

Progressive country appeared in the mid-to-late Sixties, and preceded (and influenced) outlaw music. It was singer-songwriter based, led by artists such as Kris Kristofferson, Willie Nelson, Mickey Newbury, Billy Joe Shaver, Tom T. Hall, Jimmie Dale Gilmore, Steve Earle and Butch Hancock. Others associated, though not central, to the genre were Neil Young – one of the great singer/songwriters, whose work is strongly informed by country – and The Dillards, pioneers of a 'progressive' form of amplified bluegrass.

PROGRESSIVE ANTHEMS THAT MADE THE US POP CHARTS

Harper Valley PTA (Tom T.Hall)
#1 for Jeannie C.Riley 1968

Just Dropped In (Mickey Newbury)
#5 for Kenny Rogers 1968

Ruby, Don't Take Your Love To Town (Mel Tillis)
#6 for Kenny Rogers 1969

Rainy Night In Georgia (Tony Joe White)
#4 for Brook Benton 1970

Me And Bobby McGee (Kris Kristofferson)
#1 for Janis Joplin 1971

"...my songs speak for themselves.
The musicians who play on them and the way they sound and where
they were recorded and the way they were recorded is the old Nashville
way... they sound as country or more country than a lot of things
that are on country radio... "
Neil Young

INTO THE MAINSTREAM

The sound coming out of Nashville had acquired the label 'countrypolitan' through the late Sixties and Seventies as country music moved increasingly away from its roots and country-pop became the norm. Crossover artists such as Glen Campbell (by far the most successful), Charley Pride and Charlie Rich were simultaneously topping the country and pop charts.

GLEN CAMPBELL'S BIG FIVE

Year	Title	Pop Charts Places	
1968	Wichita Linesman	US#3	UK#7
1969	Galveston	US#4	UK#14
1970	It's Only Make Believe	US#10	UK#4
1975	Rhinestone Cowboy	US#1	UK#4
1977	Southern Nights	US#1	UK#28

URBAN COWBOYS

During the early Eighties, country music was dominated by the 'urban cowboy' movement, named after the 1980 John Travolta film, that prompted a trend for

all things country and drew in a new audience for the
brand of music associated with the film – a middle-of-
the-road, rock-influenced style of country-pop.

Many felt that the result of the 'urban cowboy' boom
was a lot of shallow and gutless music that was neither
good country, nor good pop, nothing but regurgitated
Sixties and Seventies pop music.

Typical of the country-pop trend were the Oak Ridge
Boys, the vocal group whose single 'Elvira' hit the Top
Five of the pop charts and went on to earn a platinum
disc, selling over two million copies.

There were established country stars who 'crossed
over' with ease, without compromising their work –
like Dolly Parton with her '9 To 5' hit, and Kenny
Rogers with no less than 15 US Top Twenty entries
between 1977 and 1984. And new names appeared
during the Eighties who likewise bucked the trend,
being hugely successful as 100 per cent country artists,
including Barbara Mandrell, John Conlee, Alabama
and Reba McEntire.

LINE DANCE FEVER

Line dancing first became popular during the boom in
disco during the Eighties, when country fans evolved
their own dance form which could be practised in a
dance hall or club situation, without even the necessity
of a dancing partner. Although line dancing can be
applied to various musical styles soul line dancing is

particularly popular for instance – the style as it applied to country music had is roots in elements of barn dancing, which went back to American country dance of the Twenties.

After a brief craze for disco line dancing prompted by Van McCoy's soul hit 'The Hustle' – a US #1 in 1975 – country line dancing was catapulted into the public consciousness with Billy Ray Cyrus' 1992 hit 'Achy Breaky Heart'.

Even though a magazine in 2004 named his 'Achy Breaky Heart' as their choice for "the second worst song ever", Billy Ray Cyrus' success with the number was followed by six US Top Ten singles, three of which reached the #1 spot. He also holds the record for the longest time at #1 (17 weeks) for a debut album in the *Billboard* album chart, for 1992's *Some Gave All* – which also made the Top Ten in the UK album list.

POP GOES THE COUNTRY

As country music seemed to be taking on an increasingly 'pop' character in the early Seventies, the "final straw" for traditionalists came in 1974 when the British/Australian singer Olivia Newton-John was voted Female Vocalist of the Year at the CMA Awards ceremony in Nashville. So concerned were many stalwarts of the country establishment that two dozen singers – including Dolly Parton, Barbara Mandrell, Hank Snow, Conway Twitty and Faron Young – formed the rival ACE, the Association of Country Entertainers, after getting together one

November evening at the Nashville home of Tammy Wynette and George Jones.

Newton-John was just one of a number of pop-oriented "country" singers who had huge hits in the pop charts through the Seventies and early Eighties.

John Denver
Take Me Home, Country Roads
#2 pop 1971
Sunshine on My Shoulders
#1 pop 1974
Annie's Song
#1 pop 1974
Thanks God I'm A Country Boy
#1 pop 1975
I'm Sorry
#1 pop 1975

Olivia Newton-John
I Honestly Love You
#1 pop 1974
Have You Ever Been Mellow
#1 pop 1975

Bellamy Brothers
Let Your Love Flow
#1 pop 1976

Crystal Gayle
Don't It Make My Brown Eyes Blue
#2 pop 1977

Juice Newton
Queen Of Hearts
#2 pop 1981

SEXY STEAMERS

With the more liberated attitudes of the Seventies, artists often featured songs which would have shocked previous generations of mainly conservative country fans. Here are just six steamers that raised some eyebrows when they were first released.

Help Me Make It Through the Night
Sammi Smith 1970

Behind Closed Doors
Charlie Rich 1973

You've Never Been This Far Before
Conway Twitty 1973

Blanket On The Ground
Billie Jo Spears 1974

Sleeping Single In A Double Bed
Barbara Mandrell 1978

She Can't Get My Love Off The Bed
Dottie West 1982

NEW COUNTRY

In the Nineties so-called "new country" performers stormed the country and mainstream charts, a fresh breed of young Nashville artists including Clint Black, Faith Hill, Shania Twain, Alan Jackson and – the most spectacularly successful of them all – Garth Brooks.

Whereas in the early Eighties a country record was deemed a hit if it sold over half a million (earning it a gold record), by the Nineties more and more records "went platinum", selling over a millon copies. Country record sales in America in the Nineties reached nearly $2 billion, almost double the sales figure achieved in the Eighties.

Profile: Garth Brooks
Born: Troyal Garth Brooks, 7 February 1962, Tulsa, Oklahoma

Recording Debut: The album *Garth Brooks* released on Capitol in April 1989

Classic Records: 'Much too Young (to Feel This Damn Old)', 'Friends In Low Places', 'The Dance', 'Shameless', 'The Thunder Rolls', 'Two Of A Kind', 'Working On A Full House', 'The River', 'That Summer', 'Ain't Going Down ('Til the Sun Comes Up)'. Albums: *Garth Brooks, No Fences, Ropin' The Wind, The Chase, Beyond The Season*

Facts'n'Figures: Garth Brooks' second album *No Fences* reached the #4 position in the US pop charts, and the next one *Ropin' In The Wind* made it to #1 in its first week of release, selling over four million copies in the first month. Both records went on to sell over ten million copies. His singles 'Shameless', 'The Thunder Rolls', 'Two Of A Kind' and 'Working On A Full House' all made the #1 spot in the US country chart. Since the release of his debut record, he has sold over 60 million albums.

Garth Brooks' success on record was supported by a carefully cultivated image. On the one hand he wore a cowboy hat and jeans, reminding the folks that he came from Oklahoma, eschewing the glitzier dress code of the urban cowboys. But his concerts were also highly extravagant affairs, with hi-tech lighting effects, rock-style stage sets and Brooks "flying" in from the stadium rafters on cables, a head set microphone strapped across his face. A long way from the Grand Ole Opry.

Like Brooks, other "new country" singers such as Clint Black, Alan Jackson and Travis Tritt emphasised their "down home" roots, with their generally clean-cut appearance (no outlaws here) being complemented with a cowboy hat – which led to them often being referred to as "hat acts".

Female singers had an equally strong presence. Names like Shania Twain, Trish Yearwood and the Dixie Chicks dominated the "new country" assault on the mainstream charts through the Nineties and beyond.

"Country music is still your grandpa's music, but it's also your daughter's music. It's getting bigger and better all the time and I'm glad to be a part of it."
Shania Twain

NEW COUNTRY MEGA-SELLERS

Eight "new country" records featured in a list of the
Top-Selling Albums of All Time compiled by the
Recording Industry Association of America, based on
figures in mid-2005.

Artist / Album / Year / Label / Sales
Shania Twain **Come On Over** 1997
Mercury 19 million
Garth Brooks **No Fences** 1990
Capitol 16 million
Garth Brooks **Double Live** 1998
Capitol 15 million
Garth Brooks **Ropin' the Wind** 1991
Capitol 14 million
Shania Twain **The Woman in Me** 1995
Mercury 12 million
Dixie Chicks **Wide Open Spaces** 1998
Monument 12 million
Dixie Chicks **Fly** 1999
Monument 10 million
Garth Brooks **The Hits** 1994
Capitol 10 million

In 2001, the top ten most-played artists on American
radio across all genres included five country artists –
Faith Hill, Tim McGraw, George Strait, Alan Jackson
and Garth Brooks.

After Garth Brooks, the biggest commercial success
story to come out of Nashville's "new country" boom
was that of Shania Twain. Her immense popularity
came via the British rock producer (and song collabo-

rator with Twain) Robert John "Mutt" Lange, who had previously worked with (among many) AC/DC, Def Leppard, the Cars and Michael Bolton. Lange produced Shania Twain's second album *The Woman In Me*, and by the time it was released singer and producer were married.

Profile: Shania Twain
Born: Eileen Edwards, 28 August 1965, Windsor, Ontario

Recording Debut: the album *Shania Twain*, released on the Mercury label in 1993.

Classic Records: 'You're Still The One', 'From This Moment On', 'That Don't Imprss Me Much', 'Man! I Feel Like A Woman'. Albums: *Shania Twain, The Woman In Me, Come On Over, Up!*

Facts'n'Figures: In the first twelve months of its release, Shania's 1995 album *The Woman In Me* produced four Top Ten country hits in the singles charts, and went on to sell over twelve million copies. Its follow-up in 1997 *Come On Over* had sold over 19 million copies by 2005, in March 2000 having already been confirmed as both the best selling album in country music history, and the best selling album ever by a female artist.

Country is the most popular radio format in the USA, reaching 80 million adults, almost 40% of the population, every week. And the CMA International Radio Directory lists over 575 radio stations outside North

America regularly broadcasting country music, featuring both American and home-produced acts.

"I miss the tried-and-true and the dyed-in-the-wool.
I guess that's a typical comment from an artist my age.
Glory for the new artists, great. But country radio doesn't program
hardly anybody over 40. Country music is about tradition.
And they're losing that tradition. In my mind, anyway."

Johnny Cash

In 2000, 68 American country music artists toured 20 countries worldwide, the most frequently visited countries being the UK, Australia and Germany. In Australia the country music capital is Tamworth, in New South Wales, whose annual festival and awards ceremony attracts over 100 acts and 50,000 fans.

TOP TWENTY COUNTRY

The top twenty places from an internet survey of the Top Fifty Country Records of all time, taking into account *Billboard* chart positions, other charts and various surveys and polls. Patsy Cline appears twice in the top four places, and Hank Williams three times in the top ten. Merle Haggard (three times in the twenty) is the only other artist to feature more than once in the list.

1   He Stopped Loving Her Today - George Jones
2   Crazy - Patsy Cline
3   Your Cheatin' Heart - Hank Williams
4   I Fall To Pieces - Patsy Cline
5   El Paso - Marty Robbins
6   I'm So Lonesome I Could Cry - Hank Williams
7   Today I Started Loving You Again - Merle Haggard
8   Lovesick Blues - Hank Williams
9   He'll Have To Go - Jim Reeves
10 The Dance - Garth Brooks
11 Sixteen Tons - Tennessee Ernie Ford
12 San Antonio Rose - Bob Wills And His Texas
      Playboys
13 Workin' Man Blues - Merle Haggard
14 I Walk The Line - Johnny Cash
15 Mama Tried - Merle Haggard
16 Coal Miner's Daughter - Loretta Lynn
17 Old Dogs, Children, And Watermelon Wine -
      Tom T Hall
18 Always On My Mind - Willie Nelson
19 Oh, Lonesome Me - Don Gibson
20 Tiger by the Tail - Buck Owens

THE COUNTRY MUSIC HALL OF FAME

Year Inducted	Artist
1961	Jimmie Rodgers
	Fred Rose
	Hank Williams
1962	Roy Acuff
1964	Tex Ritter
1965	Ernest Tubb
1966	Eddy Arnold
	James R. Denny
	George D. Hay
	Uncle Dave Macon
1967	Red Foley
	J.L. (Joe) Frank
	Jim Reeves
	Stephen H. Sholes
1968	Bob Wills
1969	Gene Autry
	Bill Monroe
1970	Original Carter Family
1971	Arthur Edward Satherley
1972	Jimmie H. Davis
1973	Chet Atkins
	Patsy Cline
1974	Owen Bradley
	Frank "Pee Wee" King
1975	Minnie Pearl
1976	Paul Cohen
	Kitty Wells
1977	Merle Travis

1978	Grandpa Jones
1979	Hubert Long
	Hank Snow
1980	Johnny Cash
	Connie B. Gay
	Original Sons Of The Pioneers
1981	Vernon Dalhart
	Grant Turner
1982	Lefty Frizzell
	Roy Horton
	Marty Robbins
1983	Little Jimmy Dickens
1984	Ralph Peer
	Floyd Tillman
1985	Flatt And Scruggs
1986	Benjamin F. Ford
	Wesley H. Rose
1987	Rod Brasfield
1988	Loretta Lynn
	Roy Rogers
1989	Jack Stapp
	Cliffie Stone
	Hank Thompson
1990	Tenessee Ernie Ford
1991	Boudleaux & Felice Bryant
1992	George Jones
	Frances Williams Preston
1993	Willie Nelson
1994	Merle Haggard
1995	Roger Miller
	Jo Walker-Meador
1996	Patsy Montana
	Buck Owens
	Ray Price

1997	Harlan Howard
	Brenda Lee
	Cindy Walker
1998	George Morgan
	Elvis Presley
	E.W. "Bud" Wendell
	Tammy Wynette
1999	Dolly Parton
	Conway Twitty
	Johnny Bond
2000	Charley Pride
	Faron Young
2001	Bill Anderson
	The Delmore Brothers
	The Everly Brothers
	Don Gibson
	Homer And Jethro
	Waylon Jennings
	The Jordanaires
	Don Law
	The Louvin Brothers
	Ken Nelson
	Sam Phillips
	Webb Pierce
2002	Bill Carlisle
	Porter Wagoner
2003	Floyd Cramer
	Carl Smith
2004	Jim Foglesong
	Kris Kristofferson
2005	Alabama
	Deford Bailey

CONTEMPORARY COUNTRY

As well as the mainstream-friendly acts like Shania Twain and the Dixie Chicks that continue to sell records by the million, the contemporary country scene has also featured a return to the basic feel and musical values of "real" country, both in the music of the so-called "new traditionalists" and the rock-oriented, "alternative country" movement.

THE NEW TRADITIONALISTS

New Traditional country (or neotraditional as it's sometimes termed) came about as a reaction to the perceived blandness of mainstream country music, a stylistic throwback to a time when virtuosity and musical integrity were more important than image.

Emphasizing the instrumental background (and often even the dress and fashions), of country music of the Forties, Fifties and early Sixties, it looked to the elders of country music like Ernest Tubb, Hank Williams and Kitty Wells for inspiration.

Leading names in this harking back to the values of

country's golden era – without being in any way
"revivalist" – included Randy Travis, George Strait,
The Judds, Steve Earle, Lyle Lovett and Dwight
Yoakam.

Unlike alternative country, which has a rougher punk-
influenced edge to it, much neotraditional music is
considered part of the mainstream, in the instance of
artists like George Strait, Alan Jackson and Randy Travis.

As well as the Judds (mother and daughter Naomi and
Wynonna) there were plenty of other female names in
the neotraditional ranks, including Patty Loveless,
Rosanne Cash, Kelly Willis and the unique k.d.lang.

TEN TOP NAMES IN
NEOTRADITIONAL COUNTRY

Rosanne Cash (born 1955): Daughter of Johnny
Cash, her hit singlesinclude 'My Baby Thinks He's A
Train' [1981] and 1987's Tennessee Flat Top Box.
Essential album: *Seven Year Ache* [1981]

Steve Earle (born 1955): Out of the progressive
country movement, Earle brought the no-nonsense
attitude of the Outlaws into late Nineties country.
Essential album: *El Corazon* [1997]

The Judds (Naomi born 1946, Wynonna born 1964):
When Naomi bowed out due to ill-health in 1991, it
ended one of the great partnerships in modern country. **Essential album:** *Greatest Hits* [1988]

k.d. lang (born 1961): An avowed disciple of Patsy Cline who crosses over into pop areas and back again with ease. **Essential album:** *Absolute Torch And Twang* [1989]

Patty Loveless (born 1957): Mainstream-inclined singer, her voice nevertheless echoing her Appalachian Kentucky home. **Essential album:** *When Fallen Angels Fly* [1994]

Lyle Lovett (born 1957): Quirky singer whose Texas honky tonk is coloured by jazz, blues and such. **Essential album:** *Joshua Judges Ruth* [1992]

George Strait (born 1952): No-frills down-the-line country in the tradition of Merle Haggard and George Jones. **Essential album:** *Strait Country* [1981]

Randy Travis (born 1959): Traditional country with a laidback stance, delivered with an irresistably remarkable voice **Essential album:** *Storms Of Life* [1986]

Kelly Willis (born 1968): Almost-alt mix of Texas honky tonk and good ol' rock'n'roll. **Essential album:** *What I Deserve* [1999]

Dwight Yoakam (born 1956): One of the biggest talents to come out of neotraditional country, a dynamic rick-flavoured singer and seriously important songwriter. **Essential album:** *Guitars, Cadillacs, Etc., Etc.* [1986]

> *"Country music is three chords and the truth."*
> country songwriter Harlan Howard

ALT COUNTRY

Alternative country, or alt country as it's often referred to, was the result of two radically different influences from opposite ends of the music spectrum. On the one hand the traditional country music of America, exemplified by singers from the Carter Family to Hank Williams, and on the other agressive punk-influenced rock'n'roll.

Alt country is often considered a part of the broader category of Americana Music, which also takes in the edgier country & folk singers, Hillbilly Twang, modern bluegrass (or "newgrass"), Tex-Mex, and Roots Rock.

The prime pioneers of alt country are considered to be **Uncle Tupelo**, formed in 1987 in Belleville, Illinois. The group released four full-length albums during their four year recording career: the folk-punk *No Depression* [1990], *Still Feel Gone* [1991], and *March 16-20, 1992*[1992] were originally released on the (now defunct) independent record label Rockville. Their major label debut, *Anodyne* [1993], was released by Sire/Reprise.

Inspired by Uncle Tupelo's innovations, **Ryan Adams** formed **Whiskeytown** in 1994. They broke through with their second album Stranger's Almanac, before Adams left to go solo and huge success. Adam's notable albums include *Heartbreaker* [2000], *Gold* [2001], *Demolition* [2002], *Rock'n'Roll* [2003], *Love Is Hell* [2004], *Cold Roses* [2005] and *Jacksonville City*

Nights [2005], the last two as Ryan Adams and the Cardinals.

EIGHT OTHER ALTERNATIVES

The Derailers (formed 1993): Revivalist country swing
Essential album: *Reverb Deluxe* [1997]

Go To Blazes (formed 1987): Country and blues meet
    rock'n'roll
Essential album: *Go To Blazes And Other Crimes* [1995]

Wayne Hancock (born 1965): Modern rockabilly honky tonk
Essential album: *Thunderstorms And Neon Signs* [1995]

Jason & the Scorchers (formed 1981): Early example
    of country'n'punk
Essential album: *Lost & Found* [1985]

Lambchop *(formed 1988):* Quirky big band blending
    country, R&B and soul
Essential album: *How I Quit Smoking* [1996]

Son Volt (formed 1994): Electric punk, acoustic country rock
Essential album: *Trace* [1995]

Gillian Welch (born 1967): Hillbilly-influenced
    singer/song writer
Essential album: *Time* (The Revelator) [2001]

Lucinda Williams (born 1953): Country, rock and
    blues that defies category
Essential album: *World Without Tears* [2003]

BIBLIOGRAPHY & SOURCES

Betts, Graham: *Complete UK Hit Singles* [Harper Collins, UK 2004]

Brown, Tony: *Complete Book of British Charts* [Omnibus, UK 200]

Clarke, Donald [ed]: *Penguin Encyclopedia of Popular Music* [Viking, UK 1989]

Cohn, Nik: *Pop From The Beginning* [Weidenfeld & Nicholson ,UK 1969]

George-Warren, Holly: *How The West Was Worn* [Abrams, US 2001]

George-Warren, Holly: *Cowboy* [Readers Digest, US 2002]

Gillett, Charlie: *The Sound of the City* [Pantheon Books, US 1970]

Gregory, Hugh: *A Century of Pop* [Hamlyn, UK 1998]

Hardy, Phil: *The Faber Companion to 20th Century Popular Music*
    [Faber, UK 2001]

Larkin, Colin [ed]: *The Guinness Who's Who of Country Music*
    [Guinness, UK 1993]

Miller, Bill: *Cash: An Amercan Man* [Simon & Schuster, UK 2004]

Sandison, David: *Country Music on CD* [Mitchell Beazley, 1995]

Simpson, Paul [ed]: *The Rough Guide to Cult Pop* [Rough Guides, UK 2003]

Tosches, Nick: *Country* [Secker & Warburg, UK1989]

Tosches, Nick: *Unsung Heroes of Rock'n'Roll* [Secker & Warburg, UK 1991]

Unterberger, Richie: *Unknown Legends of Rock'n'Roll*
    [Miller Freeman, US1998]

Whitburn, Joel: *Billboard Book of USA Top 40 Hits* [Guiness, UK 1989]

Whitburn, Joel: *Billboard Book of Top 40 Albums* [Omnibus, UK 1991]

Wolff, Kurt: *Country Music: The Rough Guide* [Rough guides, UK 2000]

Newspapers and Magazines:

Billboard, Melody Maker, Mojo, Q, Rolling Stone

Websites

bbc.com

bmi.com

cmaawards.com

countrymusic.about.com

musicfromtheheart.com

oldtimemusic.com

pbs.org

Reuters/Billboard/entertainment-news.org

roughstock.com

scaruffi.com